Career *Think.*

Reference tool for Teens and Adults on How to Plan and Prepare for College

Takesha McClane

1/18/2016

Table of Contents

Acknowledgements

I have been very successful in all areas of my life and I owe it all to God because without him I would be nothing. I have a beautiful son who means the world to me and everything I do is for him. Although, being a single mother is tough but when I see him smile this is what keeps me motivated and encouraged. I also want to thank all of my coaches, friends and family member who helped shape my destiny.

In addition, I'm an IU alumni which is where I completed my undergrad and currently pursuing my MBA in Project Management at Columbia Southern University. In addition, to being a Professional Life Coach and a Certified Packaging Professional. I have a food and beverage background working in the areas of Micro, Quality Control, Food Safety and Packaging Engineering with both operations and corporate environments.

In short, I enjoy in my free time spending time with family and friends, camping, fishing, movies, cards, board games, traveling, working out and laughing. My passions are helping others to achieve their goals. I understand now the gifts God has given me and I will use my gifts to help others around the world. My personal goal is to begin with the end in mind with the impact I have created on many people's lives. Come one come all!

Foreword

This quick reference guide is to serve as a tool for those individuals who were not made aware of the resources available for planning and attending to college. Many individuals do not even know anyone who has went to college. This tool is designed to equip you with information you may not know or even your parents may not be made aware of. Don't wait until later, act now to jump start your education.

Unlike me, I was aware of my resources but I did not have the help of someone guiding me though the process and I had to ask a lot questions and do a lot of research. This was scary and I wasted a lot of time switching back and forth between programs because I did not have anyone to help me plan appropriately. If I had a coach to help me at the time it would have made my life so much easier.

However, I did manage to work my way through the process even with a later start then most my age. I'm now 33 years of age, with a four year old son and I have successfully completed my Bachelor's degree in General Studies and minored in Labor Studies, graduating from Indiana University of South Bend. In addition, I have also completed an MBA in Project Management from Columbia Southern University. This was hard and only by the grace of God with great mentors and coaches in my life, is how I made it.

I have coached several clients toward finding their purpose. I get feedback from clients all the time telling me how I inspired them and motivated them to plan and stay on track with their goals. I take pride in helping to shape our leaders of tomorrow. I will continue to stress the importance of education and how an individual's decision today can affect their tomorrow and for the rest of their lives. Proper planning is key. Get the tools you need now, why wait?

Chapter 1

Before graduating from high school, it's important for every student to understand the resources available to them in regards to going to college. Like many of us, most have parents do not know where to start, or even talk about college before completing high school with their children. Unfortunately, some parents feel its good enough if they can get you to graduate from high school and then from there you're on your own. Some teens do not graduate while many do not even try to go back to school to get their GED. However, you need at least your high school diploma or GED to enter college and it's never too late to go back and get either.

This is an abundance amount of concerning data around young teen's not just finishing high school or earning a GED but even going to college. There are many adults who find themselves wanting to change careers or have lost employment and need a new beginning which may mean going back to school. Just like you prepare to finish high school you also have to plan and prepare to go to college.

Making up your mind to go to college is the hardest part and the rest gets easier. Once your mind is truly made up about going to college you first need to decide what your strengths are by evaluating all of your grades you received from now until back when you were in grade school. The grades are a reflection of either the subjects you are or were good at. They also reflect the subjects you are not so good at or take very little interest in. If you're an adult and been out of school for a while you will want to pick a program in which aligns with your passions.

Once you have narrowed down what subjects you really like it's important to compare to a career assessment to make sure you have evaluated all your options before choosing a career path. A career assessment test can be found nowadays online if you just Google it, for free.

These career assessments are offered at some colleges as well.

Chapter 2

Moving forward, once you have a sense of what your strengths are understand the educational path in which you can go into based off your assessment results, now it's time to explore your different resources. Resources meaning how much money do you have to afford school and which school is right for you. Don't avoid college because you think you can't afford it you have options just choose the best options for you.

In addition, there are options such as grants, scholarships and student loans available for students to go to school. I choose a mixture of grants and student loans but if I had of known what I know now back then, I would have applied for scholarships as well in lieu of the loans.

Grants are money you get from the federal government in which you do not have to pay back. Scholarships are financial awards given to help students pay for college in which you do not have to pay back but you will have to be eligible and qualify for it based off its set criteria. Student loans you definitely have to pay back. However, these are options but there are other options. I have seen students work and pay their way through school. If you're working ask your employer about tuition reimbursement.

Chapter 3

Now, since you understand how your schooling will be funded whether it be family, yourself or the government then choosing what type of school is next. Vocational schools will teach a skill you can apply to a specific vocation such as welding for example. These schools can offer certificates, diplomas, two and four year degrees.

Colleges teach you theory, critical thinking, research and analysis and offer two and four year programs. Colleges are typically cost more than vocational schools. Vocational schools prepare you for entry level positions while colleges often prepares you for higher level jobs.

Choosing the right school with the right program based off of what you can afford is very challenging. What makes it easy is defining what program or field you want to go into. It may not matter to you where you go but rather they have your program and it fits your budget and schedule.

Schedule is important when planning for school because like many of us we have to work and take care of our families. If you're lucky you do not have to work and only need to focus on your schooling. There are options now for going to school, either in class, online or hybrid choose which option best fits your needs.

Once you have narrowed down your niche it's good to explore organizations who would hire you once you get your degree. Many top fortune 100 companies will only hire candidates from certain universities for certain roles in their organization. Be sure to explore a few companies you might want to work for if you're not leaning towards starting your own business before choosing your school.

Be sure to research the chosen university thoroughly and understanding their admission requirements to the university and the degree program. You want to understand what type or pre examinations maybe involved. Explore tuition rates, program length to understand when you will graduate and view what type of courses you will be taking to complete the program. The more you know the better off you will be.

Chapter 4

Furthermore, now that you have chosen which program you would like to enter into and have researched and found your potential vocational school or college. You can now proceed to the application process of the school of choice in order to apply their program. Sometimes there are application fees so just be prepared but the applications fees are not much. You will need to make sure you have your high school diploma or GED handy. The school can either request this from yourself or the institution in which you received your diploma from.

Once the school determines you meet the admission requirements they will send a letter of acceptance. From there you will follow your schools process on getting started with their program. Each school is different and have their own criteria's established. However, there are a few things of the process which do not change and are the same for every school in regards to filling out a free application for federal student aid, known as FAFSA. Only those individuals who are paying for their education in advance they do not have to fill one of these out.

Chapter 5

FAFSA is a process within itself and its best to do your homework on this in advance. This process is not very difficult but it can be if you do not file taxes and need your parent's tax info to determine how much student aid you will get back. There are requirements to qualify for this aid and I cannot stress to you how important it is for individuals to find out whether they meet these requirements or not. I will provide the website in a checklist down below so yourself, parent's counselor or career coach can explore.

Often times I see individuals get discouraged because their parents make too much money so they don't qualify as an independent student and postpone their education until they do. If this is the case try to apply for scholarships do not give up. I promise if you design your career appropriately you will not let anything get in the way of your purpose.

After you have applied for your FAFSA the financial aid office of your school will have you go through an "Entrance Counseling" for those who are receiving subsidized or unsubsidized loans. The counseling will explain everything in details so you are not misguided about what you are borrowing. Be sure to actually pay attention to this process since you are borrowing money that you have to repay back. Make sure to get help on this especially if it's your first time from either your counselor or career coach.

Now you understand the basics of what you need to prepare for college and how to plan for it be sure to go through this checklist to ensure you have done what you can on your part to get started. This is only a quick reference tool list, you can always customize and add to it yourself. These are just basic guidelines to get you started in the right direction.

Chapter 6

Basic Checklist Tool:

- ✓ Be sure to aim to get good grades while in high school in the areas of Math (Engineering), English (Communications) and Science (Technology)
- ✓ Career Assessments to help tailor strengths towards degree programs. Free ones can be found on Google and vocations and colleges often will have you complete one of these assessments as well. Be sure to do your research before you start your assessment this just an example, be careful of hidden fees.

http://www.assessment.com/

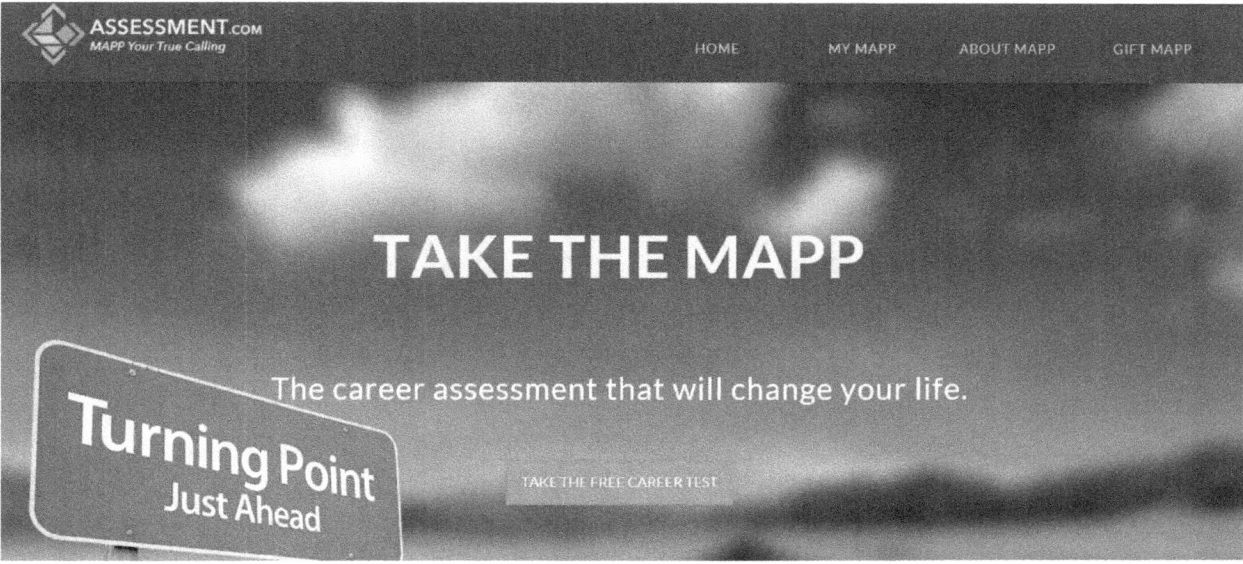

- ✓ How much can you afford or willing to spend on a quality education?
- ✓ Choice between vocational schools and colleges
  Here you can find financial information and data, this a very useful website to explore
  http://www.ed.gov/

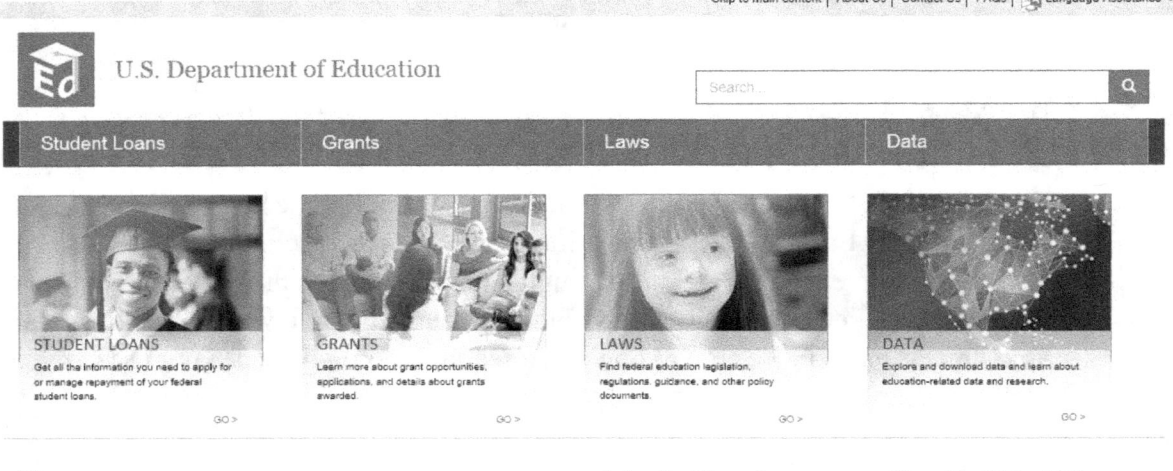

This website can give your information on predicted job outlooks and salary which help you to further decide which program is for you

http://www.dol.gov/

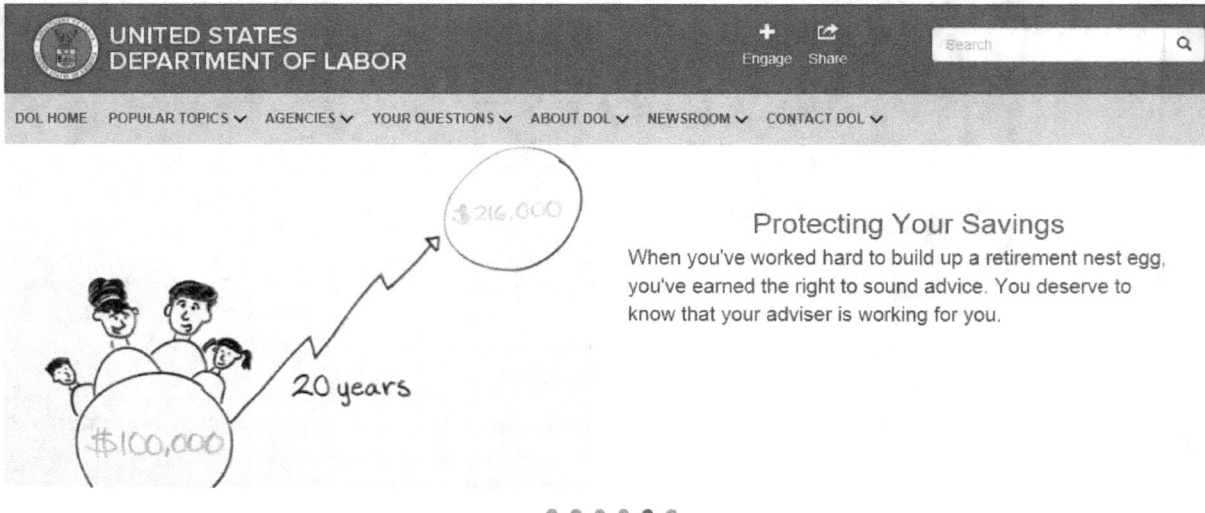

✓ Online, hybrid or in person
✓ Fill out application for school and pay any application fees if necessary
✓ Be prepared to send your high school transcripts or high school diploma to your college of choice
✓ FAFSA fill out (Fill this out at the beginning of every year typically done in Feb.)
https://fafsa.ed.gov/

✓ Student Loan Counseling
https://studentloans.gov/myDirectLoan/whatYouNeed.action?page=counseling

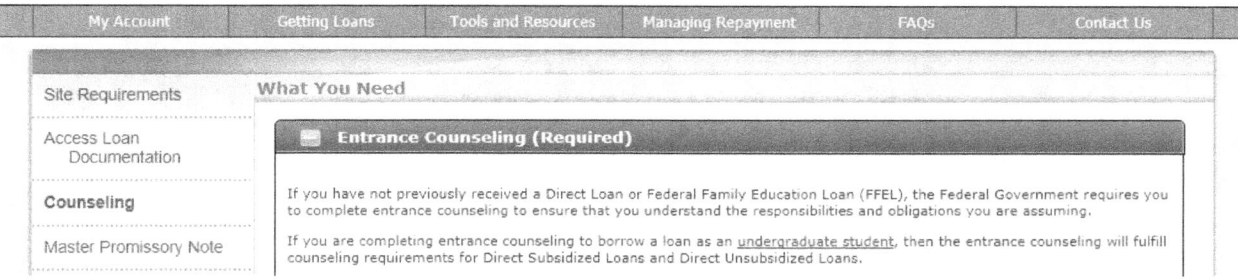

What You Need

Entrance Counseling (Required)

If you have not previously received a Direct Loan or Federal Family Education Loan (FFEL), the Federal Government requires you to complete entrance counseling to ensure that you understand the responsibilities and obligations you are assuming.

If you are completing entrance counseling to borrow a loan as an undergraduate student, then the entrance counseling will fulfill counseling requirements for Direct Subsidized Loans and Direct Unsubsidized Loans.

Chapter 7

There is more good information so please keep reading because I want to shed some light on some challenges you will face while in college and after you graduate from college. I want students to not only plan for just careers but also to become effective leaders in their careers. Many of you will go on to college and when you get there it may not be what you think and that's okay. However, just remember you are there for a reason and you have a mission to accomplish.

There are four cores I would like to encourage individuals to focus on while developing their careers because there is a particular type of character you want to have while building your personal brand. The reason why the four cores are so valuable because if you develop yourself in these areas you will much better prepared to be an effective leader which often leads to early promotions.

First, be sure to exercise if you can daily to help reduce stress and tension. Secondly, be sure to maintain a healthy and positive social group, this could friends, family and community members. Thirdly, emotionally take care of yourself keep your mind clear and continue to be a forward thinker by learning something new every day. Lastly, spiritually, build your inner core up. Your spirit is key its where most of your decisions will come from. I cannot stress to you enough how much these four cores will benefit you for the rest of your life.

Fine tune these areas, simultaneously, through your career development plan by reading books or finding a good mentor or coach who can help guide you. True success is the mastery of oneself. It's nothing worse than getting a position your character is not ready for. The four core works on developing you to become a high performing leader within the workplace. Once you have developed your core four then it does not end there. I have a question, do you want to be mediocre or reach greatness?

Chapter 8

In order to reach greatness there is a certain skill an individual needs to sharpen. This skill is called leadership. Leadership is developed and not learned. This skill is even more developed once you understand your natural abilities. There is numerous amounts of data around the most effective leadership style and the quality that individuals need to develop and possess in order to effectively lead their teams.

Since most schools do not teach you how to develop this skill its important you develop it on your own. You will stand out among your peers, often lead to quicker promotions, bonuses depending on your position. Leaders can be anyone and anywhere it does not matter if you're an entrepreneur or what position you hold within an organization. I've published articles on the importance of leadership development because I want individuals to be the best they can be. Please feel free to read down below.

Chapter 9

Moreover, get yourself a coach to help guide you through these life changing transitions to help you reach the transformation you deserve. You will constantly be revising and fine tuning your career path. Due uncertainties and unforeseen situations it may cause you to get stuck or off track and coaches can help with minimizing those risks with you.

Career and leadership coaching are essential in every aspect of your journey so utilize those resources whenever possible. I'm a professional career and leadership coach so feel free to reach out to me and visit my website at http://www.drivenpurposelifecoaching.com for all of my contact information.

I have two rules of thumb in which I live by. One, do not screw anybody on your way up. Secondly, pull someone else up when you make it. Pursue your purpose and don't let anyone get in the way of achieving it. Good luck to you and just remember, you are amazing and awesome! Down below you find a few perspective articles I have written for you to view for your own information about trends.

Get Ahead of Your Competitors with Soft Innovation

Takesha McClane

Jan. 14 2016

Companies will spend thousands sometimes millions of dollars on hard innovation projects such as technology, products and services a year and year after year. The future suggests now companies need to start working smart and begin to think about innovating without spending so much money which is called soft innovation. Tweak the small things because it's the little things that matter.

Moreover, often time when companies think about innovation its particularly geared towards processes, products, packaging, advertising, increasing quality, improving customer satisfaction etc. However, soft innovation are minor changes which do not cost a large amount of money. Soft innovation can mean sharpening the skills of your employees in order to save the business thousands of dollars.

Lastly, investing in soft innovation within the people of your organization is a key area top and middle management need to deep dive into. What you are training your employees on plays a big role as to whether or not you will see a return on investment. Career development and leadership development coaching has been an added value to organizations across the globe. How will you plan ahead to remain competitive and get ahead of your competition?

Transform the Way you do Business to Increase Profitability Through the use of Coaches

Takesha McClane

Jan 12, 2016

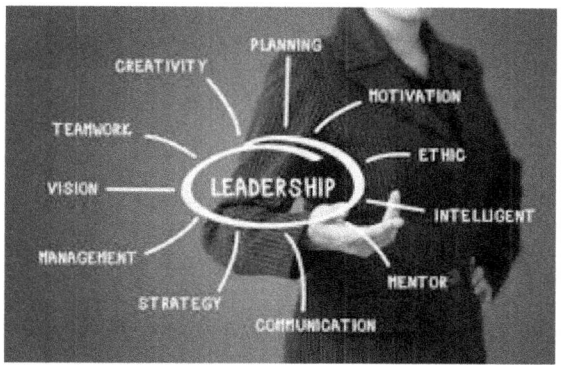

Have you ever had a bad boss and just could not stand going to work? I have and it makes it very difficult

to be productive in the workplace. It creates stress, anxiety and fear for an employee and the

productivity results of a stressed out employee is not beneficial to the organization. Poor management

can cause talent turnover, low employee morale, increased healthcare cost, lower productivity and

quality on products and services.

In addition, "The Centers for Disease Control and Prevention (CDC) reports that productivity losses linked to

absenteeism cost employers $225.8 billion annually in the United States, or $1,685 per employee." This

should not be a surprise because of the ever changing forces externally and internally due to organizations

being pressured to meet the demands of the consumers and provide quality products.

Furthermore, external pressures which drive competition within every industry is only going to get more

competitive. Macro trends display through a recent Bain study I researched on the "war for talent (Harris,

Kim & Schwedel, 2011)." Companies will be competing for talent against the young well-educated entrepreneur opportunities which means there will be less managers/bosses available in the near future

(Harris, Kim & Schwedel, 2011).

In turn, it's important for organizations to assess their current state leadership style and utilize coaches in their business to help sharpen the saw of management. Transformational leadership is by far the most sought after leadership style versus the transactional leadership style. In my opinion, I predict companies moving more towards hiring coaches in lieu of managers.

In short, coaches help transform the way people or organizations do business. Coaches motivate, empower and keeps things moving forward. Coaches are proactive and positive. Coaches are forward thinkers with growth mindsets and have the ability to inspire and influence. Coaches are trending in and bosses are falling by the way side. Get ahead of the future, start increasing profitability in your organization now, by hiring professional coaches for your business.

By Karen Harris, Austin Kim and Andrew Schwedel. September 09, 2011. *The Great Eight: Trillion-Dollar Growth Trends to 2020.* Retrieved from:

http://www.bain.com/publications/articles/eight-great-trillion-dollar-growth-trends-to-2020.aspx

Claire Greenwell. January 28, 2015. *Worker Illness and Injury Costs U.S. Employers $225.8 Billion Annually.* Retrieved from:

http://www.cdcfoundation.org/pr/2015/worker-illness-and-injury-costs-us-employers-225-billion-annually

Taking Leadership Coaching to the Shop Floor

Takesha McClane

1/11/2016

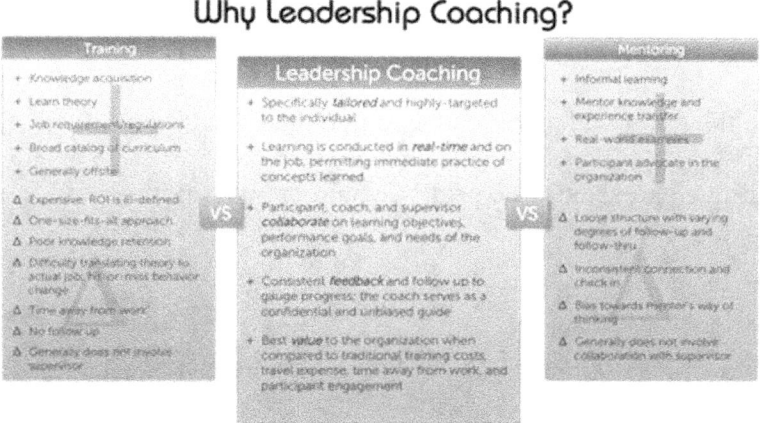

Leadership coaching, also known as executive coaching, is becoming more of a trend in today's ever changing workforce. Forbes has featured many articles on executive coaching and how it's transformed the way companies do business across the globe. This transformation has increased profitability for these companies, increased employee retention rate and has boosted morale.

While there are many definitions of leadership and coaching, mine is, "Give an individual where there is a need a preview of their vision and you have now given them purpose to drive closer towards their opportunity." In the middle of the need and opportunity is where the coaching takes place to help build and remove risks so individuals can meet their opportunity.

I have always pondered on why organizations did not utilize leadership coaching with their shop floor workers. If they did have goals they were set by their managers but they did not lead to promotion just added more responsibility and gave a few cents on the dollar for a raise. While the companies shouts how much money the company made off of their labor for the end of the fiscal year.

Individuals who work in operations are the ones who need leadership coaching the most because they are the ones getting the product out of the door. Operations are the eyes for management and they have the ability to spot out defects and catch them before leaving the facility. If CEO's and VP's recognized the dollar value which can come out of equipping their organizations with leaders starting from the shop floor, the profits would be insurmountable.

Another reason for leadership coaching on the shop floor, is there are often silos up between management and the shop floor. In every organization I have worked in, it's always been a division between those functioning units. However, it's necessary for today's workforce to be working together in every way possible to create synergy, whether you're a shop floor employee, supervisor, manager, director etc.

Just like processes need to continuously improve so does the workforce and how teams think and what they focus on. Leadership coaching is just a minor adjustment to the mindset and helps to sharpens one's sword. I do not know one company who has failed with skilled employees from top to bottom in their organization. However, I do know companies who lose a lot of money due to lack of leadership in their organizational structure from top to bottom.

In short, strengthening your operations team through leadership coaching is essential and can foster a very healthy environment. Leadership coaching will allow for the employee to identify areas to improve in and/or build upon. Having a purpose to come to work is better than coming to work just to collect a paycheck. Employees need a vision and goals to work towards so they can have a sense of purpose at work and at home. This is what everyone truly wants at the end of the day and that is to understand their purpose no matter what role they play.